TALK IT OVER

Discussion Topics for Intermediate Students

L.G. Alexander
Monica C. Vincent
John Chapman

LONGMAN INC.
New York

TALK IT OVER

Library of Congress Cataloging in Publication Data
Alexander, L.G.
   Talk It Over.

   1. English language—Textbooks for foreigners.
2. Oral communication.   I. Vincent, Monica C.,
1938-   joint author.   II. Chapman, John, 1944-
joint author.   III. Title.
PE1128.A4576   1978   428'.3'4   78-16602
ISBN 0-582-797195

First printing 1978
5

TALK IT OVER is the American English version of MAKE YOUR POINT, copyright © 1975, by Longman Group Ltd.

Acknowledgements

We are grateful to the following for permission to reproduce copyright photographs:

Monkmeyer Press Photo Service for pages 7 top (by S. Shackman), bottom right (by L. Mahon); 11 top (by H. Barad), bottom (by J. Caraballo); 15 bottom (by Hays); 49 top left (by W. Luten), right (by H. Rogers), bottom left (by D. Huffman), bottom right (by J. Caraballo). T. Lunn and K. Parker for page 7 bottom left. Syndication International for top page 15. Keystone Press Agency for bottom page 21. Camera Press for page 27 left (by P. Almasy), right (by D. Robinson). Panasonic Company for page 31. Mansell Collection for page 33.

We would also like to thank the following artists:

Martina Selway for pages 1, 25, 55. Tom Huffman for pages 3, 5, 9, 13. Mary Thomlin for pages 17, 37, 59. Michael Davidson for pages 19, 39. Robin Wiggins for pages 35, 45. Judy Sternberg for page 43. Mike Quon for page 51. Anna Veltfort for page 57.

Cover designed by Michael Vernaglia

Longman Inc.
19 West 44th Street
New York, New York   10036

Distributed in the United Kingdom by Longman Group Ltd., Longman House, Burnt Mill, Harlow, Essex CM20 2JE, England, and by associated companies, branches and representatives throughout the world.

Printed in the U.S.A.

Contents

To the Teacher

Basic Aims

There has been widespread interest in materials which give guided oral practice for students of English. *Talk It Over* is a product of this interest and has been written especially for intermediate English language classes being taught in an American English environment.

Talk It Over provides a framework through which the teacher can introduce a topic, clarify the issues involved and stimulate a discussion. Each lesson has been designed to proceed step by step in classes where students need guidance or where students are somewhat unresponsive. *Talk It Over* can also serve as a sourcebook for ideas in a class where everyone participates freely.

Most of the lessons deal with serious topics—conservation of natural resources, equal rights, how to get a job and so forth. They have been selected for their relevance to contemporary life and deal with issues which are of particular concern to teenagers and young adults. Each lesson is designed to clarify the issue in the student's mind, and enable him or her to express a cogent personal opinion about it. The format of each lesson gradually leads students into a discussion with each other.

Who the Book Is For

Talk It Over is intended for intermediate level students of English, either teenagers or adults. Since it is linguistically and culturally American, it will be particularly useful to those planning to live, work or study in an American environment.

A Description of the Material
Layout

Talk It Over consists of thirty lessons, each of which is laid out on facing pages. Introductory material (texts, photographs, cartoons and so forth) is presented on the left-hand page; exercises to guide discussion always appear on the right-hand page.

Left-hand Pages

This material is kept as short and simple as possible to enable students to concentrate on conversation rather than comprehension. Each topic is presented in an interesting manner, and the style of presentation varies from lesson to lesson. There are dialogs, picture stories, photographs, fables, letters, maps, diagrams and so forth.

Right-hand Pages

Right-hand pages are generally divided into five parts labeled **A.** through **E.** These exercises are designed to guide the student from a highly con-

trolled discussion to an open-ended discussion of the topics suggested.
A typical right-hand page takes the following form:

A. Comprehension

In early lessons, simple fact questions are used. These can be answered with short answers (*Yes, it is.*) or short, simple sentences (*He's tall.*). In later lessons, implication questions are introduced. Some of these questions may elicit a several-sentence answer.

B. Oral Composition

In this section, students are asked to construct one side, or both sides, of an argument with the aid of notes given in the book.

C. What's Your Opinion?

Here students are asked direct questions intended to get them to talk about how they personally feel about the arguments presented.

D. Talk it over.

These questions provide the basis for extensive oral work. At this point, students will begin to participate in free conversation.

E. Conclusion

This brief section gives students something to think about after class, or something to do on their own time. It may contain a quiz, a proverb, a suggested reading assignment or a piece of advice.

Time Allocation

For a class of 50 minutes, the suggested allocation of time for each lesson would be as follows:

Presentation of Left-hand Page	5-15 minutes
Comprehension Questions	5-10
Oral Composition	5-10
What's Your Opinion?	5-10
Talk it over.	5-10
Conclusion	0- 5

The first phase, presentation, is very important since the whole lesson depends on it. Some effort should be made to cover all the remaining phases during the course of the lesson. However, if a lively discussion develops in class after the presentation phase, then the lesson will have achieved its purpose even if the exercises have been only partially covered (or in some cases completely ignored). It will be found that unresponsive classes will need to go through the exercises systematically, while responsive classes will often be able to take shortcuts.

Introducing the Lesson

Two basic forms of presentation are suggested—Listening Comprehension and Interpretation.

Listening Comprehension

This method is recommended for all left-hand pages that can be read through without interruption. These are as follows:

Dialogs	Lessons 1, 3, 11, 13, 18, 23, 26, 29.
Fables	Lessons 2, 9.
Viewpoints	Lessons 6, 16, 19, 30.
Picture Stories	Lessons 7, 10, 20.

Listening comprehension introductions can be accomplished in six steps:

Step 1. (Books closed) The teacher says a few words about the subject matter. ("I'm going to tell you a story about . . .")

Step 2. (Books closed) The teacher reads (or plays the recording of) the text straight through without pauses, explanations or gestures. The students listen and try to understand as much as they can.

Step 3. (Books closed) The teacher asks a few general questions to find out how much the students understood.

Step 4. (Books open) The teacher reads the text one sentence at a time, pausing to clarify vocabulary and answer any questions which students may have. Instead of explaining everything, the teacher should try to get as much information as possible from the students themselves.

Step 5. (Books closed) This is an optional repetition of Step 2.

Step 6. (Books open) Several students take turns reading the text aloud.

Interpretation

This method is recommended for all left-hand pages which cannot be effectively presented by simply reading them aloud. These pages contain material such as photographs, maps, diagrams and so forth. They are as follows:

Photographs Only	Lessons 4, 14, 25.
Visual and Written Combination	Lessons 5, 8, 12, 15, 17, 21, 22, 24, 27, 28.

Interpretation introductions can be accomplished in two steps:

Step 1. (Books closed) The teacher says a few words about the subject matter. ("Now we're going to look at a diagram showing some career choices. Then we'll . . .")

Step 2. (Books open) The teacher reads the words (if any) aloud, and asks students to comment on the visual material. Once the literal meaning of the words and/or pictures is clear, the teacher leads the class towards an understanding of the implied meaning.

Eliciting Discussion

After introducing the left-hand page using one of the methods outlined above, the teacher presents the exercise material on the right-hand page.

A. Comprehension

Ask the questions in this section, even if similar ones have already been asked in the introductory phase. Supply additional questions of your own if you wish. Try to proceed at a fairly rapid pace. (If the class is unresponsive, it may be necessary to extend this exercise using simple questions and answers like those outlined in Section **A.**, Lessons 1-5.)

B. Oral Composition

Have the students look over the notes. Clarify anything they don't understand. Then ask two individuals to present the arguments in front of the class, or assign sections to several individuals and have "teams" present the arguments.

C. What's Your Opinion?

This exercise may be done with the whole class, or students may be directed to discuss the questions in pairs.

D. Talk it over.

Ask students to read the questions silently and think about them for a couple of minutes. Then guide the class into a discussion by asking each question. You may wish to add some questions of your own. For the most part, mistakes in grammar should be ignored, although you may wish to point out major errors after the student is finished speaking. (Some useful phrases for free discussion are found on page 62.)

E. Conclusion

Conclude the lesson by referring briefly to this section. Some of the assignments may be given as homework. The presentation steps outlined above can be abandoned altogether if a lively discussion is generated after the presentation of the left-hand page, or after any one of the sections.

Other Possible Uses

Although this book is primarily intended for guiding conversation, it may be used in a variety of other ways. Some of the texts are suitable for speed-reading or scanning. A teacher can give a dictation on the material covered, or a composition assignment based on a particular topic. Written exercises of this type are often useful in consolidating the oral/aural work done in the classroom. But it is important not to lose sight of the overall objective of the book—to develop discussion skills by presenting a range of topics which are of universal interest and concern.

1 Who'll get the job?

Interview 1.

Miss Draper: Good morning.
Please sit down. You're Ann Porter,
aren't you?
Ann Porter: Uh-huh.
Miss Draper: Which school do you
go to?
Ann Porter: . . .ton High.
Miss Draper: I'm sorry. I couldn't
hear you. Did you say Merton High?
Ann Porter: No, Burton.
Miss Draper: What's it like there?
Ann Porter: *(doesn't answer)*
Miss Draper: Well, what's your
favorite subject?

Ann Porter: I don't like any of
them, but I'm good at math.
Miss Draper: I see. Do you have
any hobbies?
Ann Porter: Not really.
Miss Draper: Then what do you do
in the evenings?
Ann Porter: Watch TV.
Miss Draper: Why do you want to
work in a store?
Ann Porter: Umm . . . I don't want
to work in an office.
Miss Draper: Do *you* have any
questions for *me?*
Ann Porter: *(shakes her head)*

Interview 2.

Bill Baker: Good afternoon. Sorry
I'm late.
Miss Draper: Good afternoon.
Please sit down. Your name's Bill
Baker, isn't it?
Bill Baker: Yes, that's right. I'm
from Parker High School.
Miss Draper: Do you have a favor-
ite subject?
Bill Baker: Yes, I do—history, but
I'm better at art. I'm not very good
at math.

Miss Draper: What are your
hobbies?
Bill Baker: I like all sports. In the
summer I swim a lot.
Miss Draper: And what do you do
in the winter?
Bill Baker: *(laughs)* I stay indoors.
I'm making my own stereo set.
Miss Draper: Why do you want to
work in a store?
Bill Baker: I think I'd like it. My
uncle has a record store. . . .

1

A. Comprehension

1. What is Ann wearing?
2. She isn't smiling, is she?
3. Has she met Miss Draper before?
4. Does Ann speak clearly?
5. Are her answers long or short?
6. What's her best subject?
7. Is she quiet or talkative?
8. Do you think she is rude, or shy?
9. Was Bill punctual for his interview?
10. He doesn't look neat, does he?
11. Does he look cheerful?
12. How does he answer the questions?
13. What's his worst subject?
14. When does he stay indoors? Why?
15. Why does he want to work in a store?
16. What questions could he ask?

B. Who'll get the job?

Here are Miss Draper's notes on the interviews:

1. *Say what she thought of Ann.*

   FOR
   a. Was punctual, neat, well groomed.
      Would look nice in a store.
   b. Good at math—would add up bills correctly.

   AGAINST
   c. Was very shy—spoke too quietly; didn't look at me.
      Seemed rude—didn't answer.
      Might be rude to customers.
   d. Seemed dull—no hobbies; no questions about the job.
      Might not work well.

2. *Say what she thought of Bill.*

   AGAINST
   a. Arrived late, didn't look neat.
      Sales help must be well groomed.
   b. Bad at math—might make mistakes in the bills.

   FOR
   c. Was very cheerful, friendly—smiled, answered questions fully. Spoke clearly. Customers would like him.
   d. Showed interest—uncle has a store. Would work hard.

C. What would an interviewer think of you?

Answer the following questions. Choose the letter that fits you best:
a. always b. usually c. often d. sometimes e. never

1. Are you neat and well groomed?
2. Are you punctual?
3. Are you cheerful and friendly?
4. Do you speak clearly?
5. Do you like meeting people?
   (Now check your score on page 61.)

D. Talk it over.

1. What would you wear to a party/to a picnic/to an interview/shopping?
2. When you go shopping, what do you notice about the sales help?
3. What can you learn about a person from his or her clothes?
4. Why are some people more shy or rude than others?

E.

Find out about jobs in stores. How much is sales help paid? Which customers do they like or dislike? What hours do they work?

2 The Foolish Frog

Once upon a time a big, fat frog lived in a tiny, shallow pond. He knew every plant and stone in it, and he could swim across it easily. He was the biggest creature in the pond, so he was very important. When he croaked, the snails listened politely. And the water beetles always swam behind him. He was very happy there.

One day, while he was catching flies, a pretty dragonfly passed by. "You're a very fine frog," she sang, "but why don't you live in a bigger pond? Come to my pond. You'll find a lot of frogs there. You'll meet some fine fish, and you'll see the dangerous ducks. And wait until you see our waterlilies. Life in a large pond is wonderful!"

"Maybe it *is* kind of boring here," thought the foolish frog. So he hopped after the dragonfly.

But he didn't like the big, deep pond. It was full of strange plants. The snails were rude to him, and he was afraid of the ducks. The fish didn't like him, and he was the smallest frog there. He was lonely and unhappy.

He sat on a waterlily leaf and croaked sadly to himself, "I don't like it here. I want to go home."

The End

A. Comprehension

1. Who once lived in a tiny pond?
2. Was it deep or shallow?
3. Were there any plants in the pond?
4. There weren't any fish, were there?
5. What other creatures lived there?
6. Why was the frog very important?
7. He was happy there, wasn't he?
8. Who passed by one day?
9. What did she ask the frog?
10. Describe the creatures in her pond.
11. Was her life boring or exciting?
12. The frog followed her, didn't he?
13. How did he get to the other pond?
14. Why was he unhappy there?
15. Where did he sit?
16. What did he want to do? Why?
17. What do you think happened to the frog?
18. Do *you* think he was foolish? Why?

B. Two points of view

1. *State the frog's point of view.*
   FOR THE SMALL POND
   a. Safe—could swim across it.
   b. Important—everyone knew him; other creatures polite.
   AGAINST THE LARGE POND
   c. Dangerous—big, deep, strange.
   d. Lonely—no one knew him; other creatures rude, unfriendly.

2. *State the dragonfly's point of view.*
   AGAINST THE SMALL POND
   a. Boring—nowhere to go, nothing to see.
   b. Boring creatures—snails, beetles; no fish or ducks. Small plants.
   FOR THE LARGE POND
   c. Exciting—dangerous ducks.
   d. Interesting—meet a lot of creatures; plenty to do, see.

C. Would you rather go to a large school or a small one?

1. *In a large school:*
   a. You study in a big building—get some exercise between classes.
   b. You go to different rooms for different classes—don't stay at one desk.
   c. You can study more subjects—there are more teachers.

2. *In a small school:*
   a. You study in a small building—don't waste time between classes.
   b. You stay in one room most of the time—don't lose things.
   c. You can learn better—have the same teachers every term.

3. Are all these points true? Can you suggest any more? What's *your* opinion?
4. Which type of school is better for young children/for teenagers/for adults?

D. Talk it over.

1. Describe your first day at a new school. How did you feel?
2. Are there any dangers in your everyday life? If so, what?
3. Describe a visit to a strange place. Was it exciting?
4. Would you like to leave home and travel abroad? Why or why not?
5. Does everyone want to be important? Would you like to be? Why or why not?
6. Do you know anything about real pond life? If so, tell us.

E. A proverb

One man's meat is another man's poison.
What are some more English proverbs?

3 Farms or **Factories?**

Mr. Hunter: Gentlemen! Listen to me, please. I've come here to help you.

First farmer: Oh no, you haven't. You want our land.

Mr. Hunter: I want to build two factories. I don't need much land for that.

First farmer: You'll take too much. And we don't want factories on our land.

Second farmer: No, we don't. Factories are ugly.

Third farmer: They're noisy.

Fourth farmer: They're smelly.

Mr. Hunter: *My* factories will give you work and money.

Third farmer: We already *have* work. We're farmers.

Mr. Hunter: How big are your farms? How much do you grow?

Fourth farmer: We grow enough to feed ourselves.

Second farmer: It's a good life.

Mr. Hunter: A good life? You work every day of the week. You never take vacations.

Second farmer: We don't need vacations.

First farmer: You can't change our lives.

Mr. Hunter: But your lives *are* changing. Where are the *young* men? Why do they leave the farms? Why do they go to the cities?

A. Comprehension

1. Does Mr. Hunter live on a farm?
2. Who is he talking to?
3. Are they friendly towards him?
4. What does Mr. Hunter want to do?
5. He doesn't need much land, does he?
6. Will the farmers give him any?
7. Why don't they want factories?
8. How could factories help the farmers?
9. The farmers don't want to change their lives, do they?
10. Are they being realistic? Why or why not?
11. Where have the young men gone? Why?
12. Would factories bring them back?

B. The arguments

1. *State Mr. Hunter's argument.*
   FOR FACTORIES
   a. Will help the farmers—work, money; regular hours, paydays and holidays.
   b. Don't need much land.
   AGAINST FARMS
   c. Very small—don't grow much.
   d. Long hours—no pay, no vacations.
   e. Young men don't like them—leave.

2. *State the farmers' argument.*
   AGAINST FACTORIES
   a. Will spoil the countryside— ugly, noisy, smelly.
   b. Will take too much land.
   FOR FARMS
   c. Belong to farmers; grow own food.
   d. A good life—like hard work; don't want to change.

C. Would you like to work on a farm?

1. Do you like working outdoors?
2. Could you get up early every day?
3. Do you like animals?
4. Are you strong?
5. Would you like to work by yourself most of the time?

If you answered *yes* to three or more questions, you'd like farming.

D. Would you like to work in a factory?

1. Do you like working indoors?
2. Would you like to work fixed hours?
3. Could you work with noisy machines?
4. Do you like working in a big group?
5. Could you do the same thing all day every day?

You'd like working in a factory if you answered *yes* to three or more questions.

E. Talk it over.

1. Do you agree with Mr. Hunter or with the farmers? Say why.
2. Have you ever visited a factory or a farm? If so, tell us about it.
3. Do you think it's important to have your own land? Why or why not?
4. Farms produce food. What do factories produce?
5. Are farmers' lives changing? If so, how?
6. What do country people want to do when they come to the city?
7. When people from the city go to the country, what do they want to do?
8. Would you rather live in a city or in the country? Why?

F. A problem

Throughout the world people are moving from the country to the cities. What difficulties does this cause? Name two or more. Is it wrong? How would *you* persuade people to stay in the country? Suggest ideas.

6

4 Boys' Work or Girls' Work?

Learning to cook

Fixing a flat tire

Using a drill press

A. Look at the photographs.

1. *Learning to cook*
   a. Was this photo taken in a home or at school? How do you know?
   b. Are the students boys or girls?
   c. Are they wearing aprons?
   d. What do you think they are making?
   e. Are they enjoying the class? How do you know?

2. *Fixing a flat tire*
   a. Who is older, the boy or the girl?
   b. What is the boy doing?
   c. Why isn't he helping the girl?

3. *Using a drill press*
   a. Where do you think the picture was taken? Why do you think that?
   b. What is she holding?
   c. Do you think she likes the work?

B. Boys and girls should learn the same things.

1. *Support this statement.*
   a. Schools should prepare students for the future—men and women will have equal rights.
   b. Both will look after children. Both will work outside of the home.
   c. So boys and girls should study same things—cooking, sewing, shop, auto mechanics.

2. *Argue against the statement.*
   a. Men and women are different—only women can have children and they should look after them.
   b. Men are stronger—they should take care of women, earn money, do heavy jobs.
   c. So schools should teach boys and girls different things— mechanical and occupational studies for boys; cooking and sewing for girls.

C. What about you?

1. *Questions for men*
   a. Can you cook?
   b. Can you sew?
   c. Do you help with the housework?
   d. Could you look after a baby?
   e. Do you think men should learn how to do these things? Why or why not?

2. *Questions for women*
   a. Can you use a drill press?
   b. Can you saw wood?
   c. Can you fix a flat tire?
   d. Could you put up a shelf?
   e. Do you think women should learn how to do these things? Why or why not?

D. Talk it over.

1. Do you think men and women are equal? Why or why not? Will they ever be?
2. Here is a list of jobs. Which can men do? Which can women do? Which can both men and women do? Can you explain why? Is it the same in all countries?
   a. salesclerk b. doctor c. secretary d. nurse e. sailor f. bus driver g. chef h. teacher i. journalist j. bank teller k. engineer l. dressmaker m. pilot
3. Should boys and girls go to co-ed schools or separate schools? Which is better for younger children? For older children?

E. Choose a present.

What would you give a boy for his seventh birthday? What would you give a girl? Why?

5 What's your verdict?

Last month game wardens caught a gang of poachers in Okaloopi State Park. They found 25 alligator skins in their cabin. The trial will take place next week. The lawyers have prepared their cases. Here are their notes.

Counsel for the prosecution

1. Poachers guilty—broke the law —no license to shoot alligators.
2. Too lazy to get jobs.
3. Killing one of the oldest animals on earth—very rare now—our country must preserve alligators.
4. Tourists come to see alligators— if they disappear the country will lose money.
5. So not only poachers, but also traitors; therefore punish them severely.

Counsel for the defense

1. Men innocent—didn't under- stand new laws.
2. Have always hunted alligators— shows they're brave.
3. Alligators take their food, eat their children, etc.
4. No jobs in that area—everyone poor.
5. Men are just tools—real crimi- nals are in the city.
6. Businessmen buy skins at low prices—make expensive hand- bags, etc., from them; sell them to movie stars, etc.—big profits.
7. Wrong men are in court—send them home; help them.

A. What are the facts?

1. Who caught the gang of poachers?
2. When and where did they catch them?
3. What did they find in their cabin?
4. When will the trial take place?
5. What have the lawyers done?
6. Is it against the law to shoot alligators?
7. Did the poachers have licenses?
8. They don't have jobs, do they?
9. Do they come from a rich area?
10. Are alligators rare or common now?
11. Why have men always hunted them?
12. Why do tourists come to see them?
13. Tourists spend money, don't they?
14. Who do the poachers work for?
15. Do businessmen pay high prices for the skins?
16. What do they make from them?
17. Who do they sell their goods to?
18. Are their profits big or small?

B. The lawyers' arguments

1. *Make the speech for the prosecution.*
   a. Why are the poachers guilty?
   b. Why don't the poachers have jobs?
   c. Why is it wrong to kill alligators?
   d. What must the country do? Why?
   e. What will happen if alligators disappear?
   f. What else are the men?
   g. What should the court do?

2. *Make the speech for the defense.*
   a. Why are the men innocent?
   b. What have they always done? Why?
   c. Why don't they have jobs?
   d. Who are the real criminals?
   e. What are the men from the park?
   f. Why do businessmen want the skins?
   g. Who should be in court?
   h. What should the court do?

C. What's your opinion?

1. If a man knows the law and breaks it, is he innocent or guilty?
2. What's your verdict in the case? Are the men guilty of poaching?
3. Do you think the men are traitors? Why or why not?
4. Do you think the businessmen are the real criminals? Why or why not?
5. If you were the judge, what would you decide? a. Punish the men severely. b. Punish the men lightly. c. Send the men home and help them.
6. If these men are punished, will the alligators be safe? Why or why not?

D. Talk it over.

1. What do you know about alligators? Have you ever seen one? If so, where?
2. Do people need alligator bags, belts, etc.? Why do they buy them?
3. Many other animals are disappearing—leopards, tigers, whales. Why?
4. Is it more important to save wild animals or to help people? Why?
5. What do tourists come to see in your country? What do they buy?

E. A problem

How can we save wild animals? Here are some ideas. Do you agree with them? Can you add any more?

1. Put all poachers in prison. 2. Punish the people who buy skins.
3. Put rare animals in zoos.

6 Down with Football

Dear Editor:

Why do people play football? It's a stupid game and it's dangerous too.
Twenty-two men fight for sixty minutes to make as many goals as they can.
They get more black eyes, bruises and broken bones than they do points.
Football players must be crazy!

And why do people watch football? They must be crazy too. They certainly
shout and scream like madmen. I'm afraid to go near a football field when
they're playing a game. The crowds are dangerous. I'd rather stay home and
watch TV. But what happens when I turn it on? They're showing a football
game. So I turn on the radio. What do I hear? The latest football scores. And
what do I see when I open a newspaper? Pictures of football players, interviews with football players, scores of football games.

Football players are the heroes of the twentieth century. They're rich and
famous. Why? Because they can run around with a ball and knock each other
down. How stupid! Everyone seems to be crazy about football, but I'm not.
Down with football, I say.

Betty Brown
Baltimore, Maryland

A. Comprehension

1. Does Betty Brown approve or disapprove of football? Why?
2. How does she describe the game?
3. In what ways is football dangerous?
4. What does Betty Brown say about football players?
5. What is her opinion of people who watch football?
6. Why can't she escape from football when she stays home?
7. Does she think football players deserve to be heroes? Why or why not?

B. Down with football?

1. *State the case against football.*
   a. Football—stupid, dangerous. Players fight, get black eyes, broken bones, bruises. Must be crazy.
   b. People who watch—crazy too. Shout, scream. Dangerous crowds. Stay home—football on TV, on radio, in newspapers.
   c. Players—heroes, rich, famous. Kick a ball. Stupid—everyone crazy.

2. *State the case for football.*
   a. Football—sensible, healthy. Better to fight on football field than in life. More danger in homes, on roads.
   b. Players—deserve fame, money —can't play when old; great skill, give pleasure to millions.
   c. Football popular—games exciting.
   d. Everyone can't go to games— TV, radio, newspapers report. Betty Brown is the crazy one!

C. What's your opinion?

1. Are *you* crazy about football? Why or why not?
2. Why do people go to football games? a. To watch a famous player. b. To support a team. c. To see the skill of the players. d. To shout and scream.
3. Do you think there is too much football on TV, on the radio and in the newspapers? Why or why not? Do you think football crowds are dangerous?
4. Do you think football players deserve to be rich and famous? Why or why not?
5. Do you think Betty Brown would enjoy watching a football game if she could play? Why do other women go to games? Should women play football?

D. Talk it over.

1. Have you ever watched a football game? What was it like?
2. Describe a famous football player. How does he play? What's his life like?
3. Have you ever broken a bone or had a black eye? How did it happen?

E. What's your score?

1. The first professional football game in America took place in a. 1856 b. 1891 c. 1901 d. 1926.
2. A football field is a. 70 yards long b. 90 yards long c. 120 yards long d. 150 yards long.
3. A touchdown gives the team a. one point b. five points c. six points d. seven points.

(Answers on page 61.)

12

7 Why are you late?

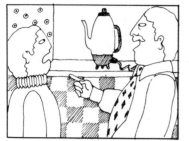

Peter: Why isn't breakfast ready?
Mr. White: Because your mother's sick. Go and call the doctor.

Peter: He's on his way.
Mr. White: Good. I'll wait for him. You'd better go to school.

Peter: (*thinks*) I'm already late. What will Mr. Jones say?

Mr. Jones: Well, good *evening*, Peter. Why are you late?
Peter: I missed the bus.
Mr. Jones: Get up earlier.
Peter: But my father...

Mr. Jones: I don't want any more excuses. You're half an hour late, so you'll have to stay for half an hour after school.
Peter: But my mother...

Mr. Jones: No excuses. You've broken a school rule. If I don't punish you today, the whole class will be late tomorrow.

Principal: Oh, Mr. Jones. You teach Peter White, don't you?
Mr. Jones: Yes, I do. He's a very good student, but he was late this morning.

Principal: I can explain that. His mother's sick and has gone to the hospital. His father just phoned.
Mr. Jones: Oh really? I'd better talk to Peter.

A. Comprehension
1. Did Peter have any breakfast?
2. Why hadn't his mother made it?
3. What did his father tell him to do?
4. Who waited for the doctor?
5. How late for school was Peter?
6. Do you think the class had begun?
7. What did Mr. Jones say to Peter?
8. What did Peter try to tell him?
9. Why didn't Mr. Jones listen?
10. Which rule had Peter broken?
11. Why did Mr. Jones think he should punish Peter?
12. Who spoke to Mr. Jones between classes?
13. What did he tell him about Peter?
14. How did the principal know?
15. Was Mr. Jones sorry to hear the news?
16. Do you think he'll make Peter stay after school?
17. What do you think he'll say to him?

B. Should Mr. Jones punish Peter?
1. FOR PUNISHMENT (before break)
   a. Peter very late—middle of class.
   b. Asked him why—missed the bus —thought he'd gotten up late. Began to make excuses—didn't listen.
   c. Had broken rule; began to argue. Must punish students who break rules—if not, every-one will be late.
   d. Teachers must be firm.

2. AGAINST PUNISHMENT (after break)
   a. Principal spoke to me during break—Peter's mother sick.
   b. Explained lateness—tried to tell me—didn't listen.
   c. Usually a good student— punctual. Must be worried, unhappy—unkind to punish him. Will talk to Peter.
   d. Teachers should be kind, fair.

C. Are you a good student?
1. Do you work hard?
2. Do you write neatly?
3. Do you get good grades?
4. Do you listen to your teachers?
5. Do you obey rules?

D. Would you be a good teacher?
1. Are you patient?
2. Are you kind?
3. Are you fair?
4. Can you explain things well?
5. Do you like to work hard?

E. Students and teachers
1. Do you think the questions in **C.** and **D.** make sense?
2. What's *your* idea of a good student?
3. What's *your* idea of a good teacher?

F. Talk it over.
1. Have you ever been late for class? What happened?
2. What are some of the rules in your school? What happens when you break one? Would you like to change any rules? If so, which ones and why?
3. If there were no rules and no punishments, would students behave?
4. What kind of rules are there outside of school? What happens to people who break them? When and why do we disregard rules?
5. Did your parents ever punish you? Why? How? Were they always fair?

G. People are sometimes unavoidably late for a date, an appointment or even with their income taxes. Describe situations in which you were late. What were the consequences?

8 Focus on Water

What's this? It *was* a river. But now you can't swim in it. It's too dirty. Fish can't live in it. There's not enough oxygen. All the birds have gone, and the plants have died. If you drank the water, you'd die too.

What happened? Factories poured waste into the river. They poisoned the water with their chemicals. Clean water goes into the factories and poison flows out. We must stop this.

A. Comprehension

1. How many fish can you see in the first photograph?
2. Are they dead or alive? How do you know?
3. Would you eat them? Why or why not?
4. Do the plants look healthy?
5. Why aren't there any birds in the first picture?
6. Would you swim in this river?
7. Would you drink from it? Why or why not?
8. Can you see a bottle? How did it get into the river?
9. Why is the river so dirty?
10. What should we do about it? Why?
11. Look at the second photograph. Are there any factories near this river? Why or why not?
12. What activities can take place here?

B. Who makes the rivers dirty?

1. *State the case against factories.*
   a. Factories dirty, selfish—use a lot of clean water, chemicals. Factory waste contains chemicals, flows into rivers, poisons water.
   b. Could clean their waste—don't —say it's difficult, expensive. Don't see dead fish, etc. Don't care—only interested in profit.
   c. Spoil rivers for everyone—can't picnic, swim, row. Soon no water to drink.

2. *State the case for factories.*
   a. Can't afford to clean waste— people won't pay higher prices —want cheap goods, not clean rivers.
   b. *Everyone* makes rivers dirty. Farmers use chemicals to grow better crops, kill insects. People throw garbage into rivers.
   c. Scientists will find new chemicals—clean rivers, use sea water.

C. How guilty are *you*?

1. What did you use water for last week? Did you waste any?
2. Have you ever thrown anything into a river or pond? If so, what? Why?
3. Do you swim, row, water-ski? If so, how dirty do you make the water?
4. Do you like hot baths and clean clothes? Would you give them up or pay more for them in order to keep rivers clean? Why or why not?

D. Talk it over.

1. Is there a river near your home or school? If so, describe it.
2. What would happen if factories couldn't use chemicals?
3. What do *you* think we can do about dirty rivers?
4. Why can't we drink sea water? What happens when oil gets into the sea?
5. If there was only a little clean water, who should have it first? (Farmers? Families? Factories? Fish?) Give your reasons.

E. Water quiz

1. What is water made of?
2. How much of your body is water?
3. How much water is used to make a. a ton of cement, b. a ton of paper and c. a gallon of beer? 1.) 60,000 gallons 2.) 800 gallons 3.) 350 gallons.

(Answers on page 61.)

9 The Boy Who Cried Wolf

Once upon a time there was a very naughty shepherd boy. He often fell asleep while he was watching his sheep. And he told lies. The villagers shook their heads and said, "That boy will come to a bad end."

One day when he was feeling bored, the boy decided to play a practical joke on the villagers. He ran down the hill. "Wolf! Wolf!" he cried. "Help! Come quickly. Wolf!" All the villagers seized their spears and ran to help him. But there was no wolf. "He heard you and ran away," the boy said. When everyone had left, he started to laugh.

Three weeks later he was feeling very bored again, and he decided to play the same trick a second time. "Wolf! Wolf!" he shouted. "Help! Come quickly. Wolf!" Most of the villagers hurried to help him. This time the boy laughed at them. "Ha, ha. There was no wolf," he said. "What a good joke!" The villagers were very angry. "Lies are not jokes," they said.

Two days later the boy woke up suddenly. He had fallen asleep in the afternoon sun. What was that big, dark animal coming towards his flock? Suddenly it seized a lamb. "Wolf!" screamed the boy. "Wolf! Help! Come quickly. Wolf!" But none of the villagers came to help him. He screamed again. The wolf heard him and licked its lips. "I like lamb," thought the wolf, "but shepherd tastes even better."

When the shepherd didn't come home that night, some of the villagers went to look for him. But they never found him.

The End

A. Comprehension
1. Was the boy in the story good at his job? Why or why not?
2. What did the villagers say?
3. Describe the practical joke the boy played one day. What happened? Why did he do it?
4. Why do you think all the villagers came to help him the first time?
5. Did they all come the second time?
6. Why didn't anyone come when the boy told the truth?
7. What happened to the boy?
8. What do you think the villagers said when they couldn't find him?
9. Did the story frighten you?
10. Would it frighten a young child?

B. Should we tell stories like this to young children?
1. *State the case for:*
   a. It's wrong to fall asleep at work, play tricks, tell lies. Children must learn this.
   b. The fable has a moral. Shepherd tells lies, wastes villagers' time. Wolf punishes him.
   c. Children like stories—listen. Don't really believe in the wolf —learn the lesson. *Every* country has fables.
2. *State the case against:*
   a. It's wrong to frighten children— hear the story—can't sleep. Dream of hungry wolves.
   b. The punishment is too severe. Some children believe the story —learn to tell the truth, but for the wrong reason—fear.
   c. Other children laugh at the story —think boy's death is a joke. Too much cruelty in the world— keep it out of children's stories.

C. What's your opinion?
1. Which moral fits the story best? Give reasons for your decision.
   a. It's dangerous to fall asleep at work.
   b. If you play tricks on older people, they won't help you later.
   c. If you tell too many lies, people won't ever believe you.
2. How do *you* think we should teach young children to tell the truth?
   a. Punish them severely when they tell lies.
   b. Tell them stories with a moral, like this one.
   c. Teach them rules like "Don't tell lies."
   d. Set a good example. Always tell the truth ourselves.

D. Talk it over.
1. Can you tell a children's story that everyone likes? Is there any cruelty in it? Does cruelty matter in children's stories? Children's films? Children's TV programs?
2. What frightened you when you were young? Tell us about it.
3. Have you ever played a practical joke? Who laughed?

E. Fire alarm
What would you do if someone suddenly screamed "Fire!"

This story was taken from *New Think* by Edward de Bono, published by Basic Books, Inc. and Avon Books, Inc. © Edward de Bono.

A. Comprehension

1. What was Bella's father's problem?
2. What did Pedro agree to do?
3. Why didn't Bella want to marry Pedro?
4. What did Pedro offer Bella?
5. What did Bella have to do? Explain.
6. What did Pedro put in the bag?
7. Who saw him?
8. What did Pedro expect to happen?
9. What would have happened if Bella had complained?
10. What would have happened if she had refused to take a pebble?
11. When Bella took a pebble, what did she do?
12. Do you think it was an accident?
13. What did Bella tell Pedro to do?
14. What color was the pebble in the bag?
15. What did this mean?
16. Why couldn't Pedro complain?
17. What do you think happened next?

B. Retell the story.

1. Give Bella's point of view. Begin: "Pedro tried to trick me. . . ."
2. Give Pedro's point of view. Begin: "I wanted to help Bella. . . ."
3. How would Bella's father tell the story?
4. Whose side are *you* on? Why?

C. Tell whether you agree or disagree with the following statements. Give your reasons.

1. Pedro was a wicked man; he sent people to prison.
2. Pedro was a kind man; he wanted to help Bella and her father.
3. Pedro was a lonely old man; he wanted to marry Bella very much.
4. Bella's father was a weak person; he shouldn't have gotten into debt.
5. Bella's father was a good man; he didn't want his daughter to starve.
6. Bella was very clever; she found the answer to a very difficult problem.
7. Bella was dishonest; she tricked Pedro.
8. Bella was foolish; sensible girls marry rich men.
9. Women should marry for love, not money.
10. Fathers have a right to choose their daughters' husbands.
11. If people trick you, it's all right to trick them.
12. The end justifies the means.

D. Talk it over.

1. What kind of person would you like to marry? Describe your ideal partner.
2. Why do people sometimes need to borrow money?
3. If you needed to borrow money, what would you do?
4. Have you ever had to make a difficult decision? What was the problem? What did you do?
5. Can you tell a story in which someone plays a clever trick?

E. Two proverbs

Neither a borrower nor a lender be.
True love finds a way.

11 Too Old at Twenty

Do you remember Sally Green, the swimming champion? She was the girl who broke all the records at the last Olympics. Where is she now? Last week, our reporter, Tom Parker, went to see Sally at her California home.

Tom: Is it true that you don't swim at all now?
Sally: I'm afraid so. I'm too old.
Tom: But you're only twenty!
Sally: That's too old for a swimmer. If I swam in an international competition now, I wouldn't win. So I'd rather not swim at all.
Tom: But don't you enjoy swimming?
Sally: I used to, when I was younger. But if you enter the big competitions, you have to work very hard. I used to get up at 6 A.M. and go to the pool. I had to train before school, after school and on weekends. I swam 35 miles every week!

Tom: But you were famous at fifteen. And look at all those trophies!
Sally: Would *you* like to polish them? It's true that I have some wonderful memories. I enjoyed visiting other countries, and the Olympics were very exciting. But I missed more important things. While other girls were growing up, I was swimming. What can I do now?

A. Comprehension

1. What is Tom Parker's job?
2. Why was Sally famous at fifteen?
3. What country does she live in?
4. Why doesn't she swim anymore?
5. What did she dislike about her life as an international swimmer?
6. Why is the reporter surprised?
7. What does Sally think of her trophies?
8. What are her best memories?
9. What do you think "I missed more important things" means?
10. Does she have any plans for the future?

B. What is life like for a swimming champion?

1. *State the advantages.*

    a. Famous at an early age—everyone knows you; people want to meet you; reporters interview you; picture in newspapers, magazines.

    b. Exciting life—visit other countries; swim in big races; break records.

    c. Rewards—prizes, trophies, wonderful memories.

2. *State the disadvantages.*

    a. Famous too young—no social life; miss the things other girls do; reporters ask silly questions; can only win races when young.

    b. Hard life—have to get up early; train for hours; swim miles; don't enjoy the sport anymore; don't see much when traveling.

    c. Can't live on memories—no future.

C. What's your opinion?

1. Is it more important to enjoy swimming or to win races?
2. Do you think Sally was right to give up swimming? Why or why not?
3. How would you describe a "normal" life for a girl of fifteen?
4. Do you think it's a good idea to visit other countries when you're young? Why or why not? Would *you* like to travel?
5. What advice would you give Sally? When will *you* be too old to enjoy life?

D. Talk it over.

1. What can you tell us about the Olympic Games? When did they first start? Where are they held? Name some of the events. Name some record holders.
2. Why do people try to break records? What is the point of trying to swim faster or run faster than someone else?
3. Why do swimmers and other athletes have to train so hard?
4. Talk about some famous athletes in your country.
5. Here are some famous names: Columbus, Beethoven, Lincoln, Edison. When did these men live? What nationality were they? What did each man do?
6. Do people always have to work hard to become famous? Why or why not?
7. Are young people often famous? Why or why not?
8. Why are there more famous men than women? Name a famous woman. What is she famous for?

E.
Read a magazine article, an encyclopedia entry or a book about a famous person. Report to the class on how and why the person became famous.

12 A Good Alibi?

Lt. Lacey: Good afternoon, Joe. Do you have any news on that robbery in Bayside?

Sgt. Summers: Yes, sir. I got a statement from Bates, but he's got a good alibi. Here it is.

Statement

On Wednesday, March 8, 1978, I, John Arthur Bates, went to see my sister, Mrs. Elizabeth Brown. It was her birthday. She lives in Smithtown. I left my house on 70th Street soon after 9 a.m. The mailman saw me. My car is a red Ford, license number GP 144. I took the expressway from Manhattan to Long Island City where I filled up with gas. I had some breakfast at the Sunshine Diner in Rego Park. The waiter told me there had been an accident on the expressway near Fresh Meadows. Two pilots were driving to Manhattan from the airport and they hit a truck. The road was still blocked so I took the parkway to Westbury where I stopped at the Farmers' Market to buy some flowers for my sister. Then I continued on the parkway to Smithtown. I reached my sister's in time for lunch at 12 o'clock. It was a seventy-five-mile trip.

Signed:

John A. Bates

Sgt. Summers: I've checked his alibi with the mailman, the man at the gas station and the waiter in the diner. There *was* an accident on the expressway and the flowers are still in his sister's house.

Lt. Lacey: Hmmmm, Bring me the Sunday paper. Look up the Farmers' Market advertisement and then look at the map. He *could* have gone to Bayside.

A. What happened?

1. Had there been a robbery or a murder in Bayside?
2. Which policemen were dealing with the case?
3. What did Sgt. Summers get from Bates?
4. What did Sgt. Summers think of Bates's alibi?
5. What did Lt. Lacey think?

B. Check Mr. Bates's alibi using his statement, the map and the newspaper advertisement.

1. Where is Bates's home?
2. Why did he go to see his sister?
3. What day of the week was it?
4. Who saw him leave?
5. What kind of car does he have?
6. Which road did he take first?
7. How far is it from Manhattan to Smithtown?
8. What was Bates's average speed?
9. How many times did he stop? What did he do? Who did he speak to?
10. Why didn't he go through Fresh Meadows?
11. Where did he buy some flowers?
12. Which road goes directly to Smithtown?
13. Could Bates have taken Northern Blvd. from Manhattan? Why or why not?
14. Which road is Bayside on?
15. How can you get from Rego Park to Bayside?
16. Can Bates prove he went to Westbury?
17. Where did he say he'd stopped between Rego Park and Smithtown?
18. When is the Farmers' Market open?

C. Would you make a good detective?

1. What do you think of Bates's alibi?
2. What other questions would you ask him?
3. Which towns would you visit?
4. Which stores would you go to?
5. Who would you interview?
6. What questions would you ask?
7. How could you find out if Bates had taken the parkway or not?
8. How would you find other suspects?
9. Read the conclusion on page 61. Do you agree with it? Why or why not?

D. Talk it over.

1. Is it easy to remember exactly what you did on a certain day? What did you do three weeks ago today? Could you state every detail?
2. What are the most common crimes in your country? Is it easy to catch criminals? Why or why not?
3. Would you like to be a detective? Why or why not? What else do policemen do?

E. Play a game: Alibi.

1. Suggest a crime. For example, someone stole a car at lunchtime on Monday.
2. Choose two "suspects." Send them outside the classroom to make up an alibi.
3. Prepare some questions to ask the suspects. For example, "What were you doing at lunchtime last Monday?"
4. Call in one suspect and interview him or her. Then call in the second person and ask the same questions. If they both give the same answers, they are innocent; if they give different answers, they are guilty.

13   Music or **Money?**

Mr. Davis: (*quietly*) Why aren't you doing your homework?
Martin: I'll do it later, Dad. I have to get these chords right first. Our group's giving a concert on Saturday.

Mr. Davis: (*laughs*) Oh, are you? You'll be making records next, I suppose?
Martin: We hope so. The man from Dream Discs is coming to the concert so I want to play really well.

Mr. Davis: You'd better finish your homework. You can practice all day Saturday.
Martin: Oh, Dad. You don't understand at all. This concert could change my life.

Mr. Davis: It certainly could! You've got exams next month. Important ones. If you don't get a diploma, you won't get a decent job.
Martin: (*rudely*) I don't need a diploma to play the guitar. And I don't want a boring old job in a bank anyway.

Mr. Davis: (*angrily*) Oh, you don't? Whose boring old job paid for this house? *And* for that guitar?
Martin: (*sighs*) I know, yours did. But *I'd* rather be happy than rich.

A. Comprehension
1. What was Martin doing when his father came in?
2. Why wasn't he doing his homework?
3. Was Mr. Davis pleased or annoyed?
4. Why did Martin think the concert on Saturday was important?
5. Why did his father disagree?
6. Where does Mr. Davis work?
7. Why doesn't Martin want to work in a bank?
8. What made Mr. Davis angry?
9. Why do you think Martin was rude?

B. Give the arguments.
1. *What did Mr. Davis tell his wife?*
   a. Worried about Martin—playing the guitar, not doing homework. Dreaming of concerts, records.
   b. Exams next month—if he fails, no diploma, won't get a good job.
   c. Doesn't understand why a good job is important—good pay, security.
   d. Rude to me—called my job boring. Ungrateful—house, guitar. Stupid—doesn't want to be rich.

2. *What did Martin tell his friends?*
   a. Dad angry with me—practicing the guitar, not doing homework.
   b. Concert Saturday—man from Dream Discs—change my life. Dad talks about homework, exams, jobs.
   c. Want to be a musician, not a bank clerk—interesting, exciting life.
   d. Dad doesn't understand—talks of money, security. I'd rather be happy.

C. Would you like to work in a bank?
1. Are you good at math?
2. Are you careful in all your work?
3. Would you like a secure life?
4. Are you willing to take more courses?
5. Would you like a five-day week?

If you said *yes* to the first question and at least two others, you'd like working in a bank.

D. Would you like to be a musician?
1. Can you play an instrument well?
2. Would you like to work on weekends?
3. Could you stand financial insecurity?
4. Do you like traveling?
5. Could you stand irregular hours?

If you answered *yes* to the first question and at least two others, you'd like being a musician.

E. Talk it over.
1. Do you agree with Martin or with his father? Give reasons.
2. What are your views on homework? Does it interfere with your hobbies?
3. Can you play a musical instrument? Do you practice enough? Why or why not?
4. Who is your favorite musician? What is your favorite record? Why?
5. Are there any secure jobs for musicians? If so, what?
6. Suggest some jobs for which you need a diploma. Are they the best jobs?
7. Would you rather have the same job for many years, or would you like to change from time to time? Give your reasons.
8. Is it easy for children and parents to understand each other? Why or why not?

F.
Find out how much the following people earn: a bank clerk; a bank manager; an ordinary musician; a famous rock star.

14 Too Much ... Too Little ...

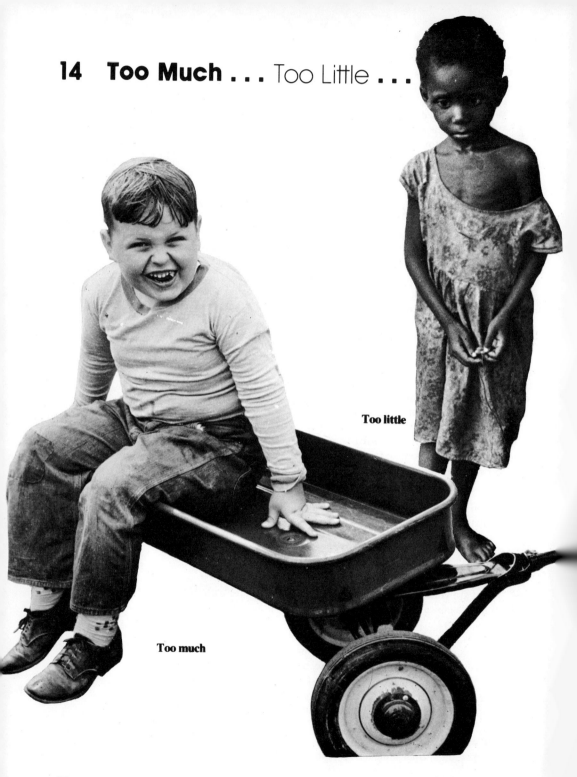

Too little

Too much

A. Look at the pictures.

1. *Too much*
  a. Is the boy fat or thin?
  b. How old do you think he is?
  c. What's he doing?
  d. Does he look happy or sad?
  e. Is he from a rich country or a poor one? How can you tell?
  f. Do you think he gets too much to eat? Why or why not?

2. *Too little*
  a. Does the child look happy or sad? Why?
  b. Do you think she ever gets enough to eat?
  c. She's from a poor family, isn't she?
  d. Is she from a rich country?
  e. Why isn't she playing?
  f. What do you think her future will be like?

B. Children today have too much to eat.

1. *State the argument.*
  a. Too many fat children—eat too much; large meals, cookies, candy.
  b. Fat people are unhealthy—more diseases; die young.
  c. Children should have a sensible diet—eat to live, not live to eat.

2. *State the counter-argument.*
  a. Many children are starving—too little food; droughts, famines in some countries.
  b. Many children are ill—don't get the right food.
  c. Children in poor countries are dying—rich countries should help.

C. What's your opinion?
  1. Do you think children today eat too much? Do *you* eat too much?
  2. Do you think candy and cookies are bad for you? How much of these foods do you eat every week?
  3. Would you rather be fat or thin? Give your reasons.
  4. How can starving children best be helped? Should rich countries give food to poor countries? Why or why not?
  5. Look over this list of foods: milk, meat, cake, bread, cheese, fish, chocolate, eggs, rice, oranges, beans, ice cream, potatoes, cabbage, coffee, tea, butter. Which foods contribute to good health? Which ones are not essential to good health?

D. Talk it over.
  1. Describe the best meal you've ever had.
  2. Has there ever been a bad drought in your country? If so, tell what happened.
  3. Have you ever seen pictures of starving children? If so, where? What country were they from? Was there a famine?
  4. Do you know where *your* food comes from? If so, tell us.

15 Finding the Right Job

accountant **sailor** **musician** **nurse** **mechanic**	**fashion model** **lawyer** **secretary** **beautician** **social worker**	**editor** **machine operator** **salesperson** **teacher** **photographer**

The chart below shows the academic skills, work preferences and personality traits of three students. The fourth column is blank so that you can check off the items which apply to you. Try to choose two items under each heading. If you have a special interest or ability, enter it in the space at the bottom.

	Peter Dent	Paul Hart	Mary West	(You)
Academic Skills				
math, science		✓		
language arts	✓		✓	
manual arts		✓		
social science	✓			
office skills			✓	
Work Preferences				
with individuals			✓	
with groups	✓			
with machines		✓		
with facts	✓		✓	
with problems		✓		
Personality Traits				
quiet, shy		✓		
responsible				
open, friendly	✓		✓	
good at details	✓	✓		
assertive			✓	
Special Interest	*children*	*cars*	*travel*	

A. Comprehension

1. *Look at the list of jobs.*
   a. What does an accountant do?
   b. Where does a nurse work?
   c. What do lawyers do?
   d. Which people probably work at night?
   e. Which people travel as part of their jobs?
   f. Which jobs require a high school education?
   g. Which jobs require a college education?
   h. Which jobs involve the use of machines?

2. *Look at the chart.*
   a. What are Peter's best subjects in school?
   b. What are his work preferences?
   c. What is his personality like?
   d. What special interest does he have?
   e. What can you say about Paul Hart?
   f. Describe Mary West.
   g. What subjects do you do best in?
   h. What are your work preferences?
   i. Describe your personality.
   j. What's your hobby or special interest?

B. Suggest several jobs for each person.

1. Peter Dent—good in language arts, social science; likes to work with groups; is responsible and friendly, pays attention to detail; is interested in children. Would make a good teacher.
2. Paul Hart—good in science, manual arts; likes working with machines and problems; is shy and detail-oriented; has a special interest in cars. Would make a good mechanic.
3. Mary West—best subjects are language arts and office skills; likes to present facts and work with individuals; is friendly and assertive; wants to travel. Would probably be happy as a saleswoman.

C. What's your opinion?

1. Do you agree with the suggestions in **B**? Why or why not?
2. What jobs should each one *not* choose? Why?
3. Describe your own abilities, preferences and interests. What kind of job do you think you would be good at? Why?
4. What jobs *wouldn't* you like? Why? What personality traits are necessary in order to do these jobs well?
5. Would you like to have the same job all your life? Why or why not?

D. Talk it over.

1. Describe a day in the life of a mechanic. A saleswoman. A musician.
2. How can you get specific information about different jobs?
3. Who is the best person to advise you when you're choosing a job?
4. Name some additional factors which are important in the choice of a job. What about money and working hours?
5. Can people change their abilities? What about their personality traits?

E. How does this statement apply to finding a job?

A square peg doesn't fit in a round hole.

16 Stop the Electronics Monster!

Dear Editor:

Why do newspapers carry so many advertisements for electronic equipment? Last Sunday I counted ads for seven different brands of televisions and 13 kinds of radios in the *Atlanta Journal.* Besides that, there were pages and pages of ads for Citizens' Band radios, stereos and tape recorders.

Don't you realize what electronic devices are doing to our daily life? Everywhere you go radios are blaring music and advertisements; this continual noise is ruining our ears. Husbands don't talk to wives anymore; they're always watching the news or a ball game. Children ruin their eyes (not to mention their minds) with endless hours of watching violent programs. When there *is* a decent program on, CB radios often ruin the reception. And worse, hidden microphones find out about our private lives, and computers handle personal information about us.

Enough is enough! I think you should limit the amount of advertising of electronic equipment in the *Atlanta Journal.* You can help stop this monster before it makes life unbearable for us all.

Jason Collins
Atlanta, Georgia

A. Comprehension
1. What is Jason Collins upset about?
2. How many radio and television ads were in last Sunday's newspaper?
3. What problem does Jason Collins think radio causes?
4. What bad effects does television have on children?
5. What is his complaint against CB radios?
6. What kinds of equipment invade our private lives?
7. What does Jason Collins think the *Atlanta Journal* should do?
8. What will happen if the "monster" is not stopped?

B. Two points of view
1. *Electronic equipment causes problems.*
   a. Television—people don't talk, marriages break up; children ruin eyes, learn to be violent; waste of time for everyone.
   b. CB radio—interferes with regular radio and television broadcasts; enables drivers to ignore speed limits by locating police cars.
   c. Computers—keep records of personal information about us, give it to strangers; make us less human, we talk to machines not people; computers make mistakes, not perfect.

2. *Electronic equipment brings benefits.*
   a. Television—educates, gives news of the world, information about foreign countries; cheap, convenient entertainment.
   b. CB radio—helps motorists in distress; can report emergencies; enables users to make new friends.
   c. Computers—help doctors cure people; help police find criminals; make possible space travel.

C. What's your opinion?
1. Do you agree with Jason Collins? Why or why not?
2. Do you think that newspaper advertisements make people buy more radios and televisions? Why or why not?
3. What kinds of electronic equipment do you own? How are they beneficial? What problems do they cause?
4. Do you think computers should be allowed to have personal information about all citizens? Why or why not? What kinds of information shouldn't computers have? Why?

D. Talk it over.
1. Has an electronic device ever made you angry? If so, describe what happened.
2. How do electronic devices save lives? Has a family member or friend ever been saved by such a device?
3. How much television do you watch every week? Do you think most programs you watch are valuable? Do you feel you watch too much television?
4. What kinds of electronic equipment would you like to own? Why?
5. Some people think radio and television are unnecessary. Could *you* live without them? How would your life be different?

E. Which of the following devices was invented first? Second? Third?
Fourth? a. telegraph b. television c. radio d. telephone   (Answers on page 61.)

17 Focus on Success

What makes a man successful? The experts think they have an answer. He must grow up in a good home. The seeds of success are sown in childhood. Some children are unlucky. They grow up in poor homes. Their parents can't get jobs, so their families never have any money. They live in small, crowded homes and don't get enough to eat. Their parents are often ill and sometimes die. They can't afford to go to school, so they aren't properly educated. They don't have a chance.

Let's look at an example:

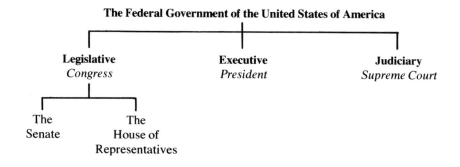

Date of birth:	February 12, 1809
Place of birth:	U.S.A.
Father:	Farmer. Moved frequently.
Mother:	Died when he was nine. Brought up by stepmother.
Home:	One-room cabin. Dirt floor.
Education:	One year of school.
1828:	Went to Illinois alone. Took various jobs: a. storekeeper, b. laborer, c. postmaster. Borrowed books and read all night. Taught himself law.
1834:	Elected to the State of Illinois Legislature.
1847:	Seat in U.S. Congress.
1861-1865:	President of the United States.
Died:	April 15, 1865

According to these experts, Abraham Lincoln didn't have a chance. What made *him* successful? Could the experts be wrong?

The Federal Government of the United States of America

Legislative	Executive	Judiciary
Congress	*President*	*Supreme Court*

The
Senate

The
House of
Representatives

A. Comprehension

1. Are some people more successful than others?
2. Why? What do the experts say?
3. Why are some children unlucky?
4. What do the experts mean by "a poor home"?
5. Does the writer agree with them?
6. Where was Lincoln born? How long ago?
7. What did his father do?
8. What happened to his mother? Who brought him up afterwards?
9. What was his home like?
10. How much education did he get?
11. Do you think he had a good start in life? Why or why not?
12. Where did he go in 1828?
13. What jobs did he get? Were they good ones?
14. How did he spend his free time?
15. Who taught him law?
16. Describe his political career. What happened in 1834? In 1847? In 1861?
17. Would you say he was successful? Why or why not?

B. What makes a person successful?

1. *Summarize the experts' argument.*
   a. Seeds of success—childhood. Successful people—good homes.
   b. Some children unlucky—poor homes; parents no job, no money; parents get sick or die.
   c. Homes—small, crowded. Not enough food.
   d. No school, poor education— don't have a chance.

2. *Summarize a counter-argument.*
   a. Many successful people—poor homes; want to escape poverty, prove themselves. Work hard, teach themselves.
   b. Parents no money—but kind, honest; help children, love them.
   c. Rich parents spoil children— lazy; don't work; fail.
   d. Experts only notice money— ignore ability, desire to succeed.

C. What's your opinion?

1. Do you agree with the experts' argument or with the counter-argument? Why?
2. Do you think Abraham Lincoln was typical of people from "poor" homes, or was he an exception?
3. Are all children of rich parents spoiled and lazy? Give examples.
4. What are the most important things parents can give children?
5. What does the writer mean by success? What do *you* think it is?

D. Talk it over.

1. Describe your idea of a good home and a happy childhood.
2. What is meant by success in school life? Do you know anyone who failed in school but became successful later? What problems can success bring?

E. A proverb

If at first you don't succeed, try, try again.

18

Should students take part-time jobs?

Moderator: This month our television panel looks at part-time jobs. Are they good for students or not?

Principal: Definitely not. Students have two full-time jobs already: growing up and going to school. Part-time jobs make them so tired that they fall asleep in class.

Mrs. Barnes: I agree. I know school hours are short, but there's homework to do. And growing children need a lot of sleep.

Mr. Barnes: *Young* children perhaps, but students usually stay in school until they're seventeen or eighteen. A part-time job can't harm them. In fact, it's good for them. They earn their own spending money instead of asking their parents for it. And they see something of the world outside of school.

Businessman: You're absolutely right. Students learn a lot from a part-time job. And don't forget that some families need the extra money. If young people didn't take part-time jobs, they couldn't stay in school.

Moderator: Well, we seem to be equally divided: two for, and two against. What do our viewers think?

Principal

Mr. Barnes

Businessman

Mrs. Barnes

A. Comprehension

1. Who are the members of the panel?
2. Why do you think they were chosen?
3. What are they discussing?
4. Why does the principal think part-time jobs are bad? Who agrees?
5. What point does she add?
6. Does her husband agree with her?
7. What's his opinion about part-time jobs for older students?
8. Does the businessman agree with Mr. Barnes or with the principal?
9. In what ways does he think part-time jobs are useful?
10. How is the panel divided?

B. Should students take part-time jobs?

1. *State the case for part-time jobs.*
   a. Good for older students—earn spending money; don't ask parents. See the world; learn a lot.
   b. Help their families—extra money.
   c. Help themselves—can afford to stay in school.

2. *State the case against part-time jobs.*
   a. Bad for young people—two jobs already: growing up, going to school.
   b. Children—a lot of sleep; part-time jobs—tired, sleep in class.
   c. School hours short, but homework. Education important, not money.

C. What's your opinion?

1. Is growing up a job? Why or why not? Is going to school a job?
2. Do all students need a lot of sleep? Why do some students fall asleep in class?
3. Is it better to earn spending money or to have someone give it to you? Why?
4. What can you learn from a job that you can't learn in school?
5. Part-time jobs can be done at different times: before school, after school, on weekends, during vacations. What are the advantages and disadvantages of working at each of those times?
6. Here are some part-time jobs: washing cars, working in a store, baby-sitting, taking care of lawns. If you wanted a part-time job, which one would you choose and why?

D. Talk it over.

1. Have you ever fallen asleep in class? What happened?
2. What are the advantages and disadvantages of staying in school until you graduate?
3. In most countries it is more common for college students than for high school students to take part-time jobs. Can you suggest reasons why?

E. A problem

Mario is sixteen and very intelligent. His teacher thinks he can get a college scholarship. But his father is sick and there are three younger children. If Mario left school, he could get a job and help his family. Should he leave school or not? What do *you* think?

19 Why can't I do what I want?

More people live to 80

What's wrong with today's youth?

Sandra Kirk's English teacher asked the class to write a composition on this topic: *The Generation Gap*.

I hope I never grow old. My grandfather lives with us and he's making my life miserable. When I was young, he was kind and cheerful. Now he's always complaining and criticizing. I'm not allowed to interrupt when he's talking. He's the one that's rude! He doesn't like my clothes. "Nice girls don't dress like that," he says. "You shouldn't wear makeup. Natural beauty is best."

Sometimes he interferes with my homework. "When I was young, we did math differently," he says. He's so old he doesn't know anything. He doesn't like my friends or my favorite records. "You're making too much noise," he yells. "I can't sleep."

When he's not complaining, he's asking questions. "Where are you going? Where have you been? Why aren't you helping your mother?" He thinks I'm six, not sixteen. Why can't I do what I want? It's *my* life, not his.

A. Comprehension

1. How old is Sandra?
2. Why doesn't she want to grow old?
3. How has her grandfather changed since she was young?
4. Why does she think he's rude?
5. Why does he think she's rude?
6. What are his views on makeup?
7. Why can't he do her math?
8. Why does Sandra think he shouldn't criticize her?
9. Why doesn't he like her friends?
10. What keeps him awake at night?
11. What questions does he ask Sandra?
12. Why does this make her angry?
13. Do you think Sandra makes her grandfather happy? Why or why not?

B. Two points of view

1. *State Sandra's point of view.*
   a. Hope never grow old—grandfather making life miserable. Young—kind, cheerful. Now—complaining, criticizing.
   b. Not allowed to interrupt—he's rude. Doesn't like my clothes, makeup.
   c. Interferes with homework—math different. So old he knows nothing—but criticizes me.
   d. Dislikes friends, records—too much noise; can't sleep.
   e. Asking questions—*my* life.

2. *State her grandfather's point of view.*
   a. Old—live with son and family. Sandra—used to be quiet, polite; now doesn't listen, interrupts.
   b. Granddaughter wears terrible clothes, too much makeup—not nice, natural.
   c. Try to help her with homework—math difficult now.
   d. Try to like her friends, records—noisy, can't sleep.
   e. Worries her mother—doesn't help; goes out, doesn't say where. Rude, inconsiderate, selfish girl.

C. What's your opinion?

1. How could Sandra and her grandfather be happier?
2. Why do old people and teenagers have different views on clothes, music, etc.? Who's right?
3. Are *you* looking forward to growing old? Why or why not?
4. Are the following statements true or false? Give your reasons.
   a. Old people don't know anything.
   b. Life is easier for old people than it used to be.
   c. Grandparents spoil their grandchildren.
   d. Three generations can't live in the same house.

D. Talk it over.

1. In some countries, old people live alone or in hospitals. Do you think this is right? Why or why not? What's the best way to look after old people?
2. Is it fair to keep other people awake? What happens in your family?
3. What would happen if everyone did what they felt like doing?

E.
Find out how your grandparents lived when they were teenagers. Describe their clothes, music and social lives.

20 Forget It?

A. Comprehension

1. When was the soccer game?
2. Why did Mary go?
3. Describe Paul. How did he play?
4. When and where did he arrange to meet Mary?
5. What did Mary see when she arrived?
6. What did she ask Paul?
7. What did Paul reply?
8. Why did Mary stop asking questions?
9. Where did Paul and Mary have dinner?
10. What did Mrs. Cobb think of Paul?
11. What did Kate show Mary on Monday?
12. Who did people suspect? Describe him.
13. Why did Kate think he might be the thief?
14. Why was Mary worried?

B. What should Mary do?

1. *State the reasons for going to the principal.*
   a. Met Paul after game—hand on wrong coat; put something in pocket; wouldn't answer her; angry.
   b. Could have been John Brooks's coat; could have put $5 in pocket; behaved in a guilty way.
   c. People suspect Jimmy Barker—not popular; call him a thief. He's crying; says he's not.
   d. Jimmy could be innocent; Paul could be guilty. Mary knows something.

2. *State the reasons for not going to the principal.*
   a. Paul—nice boy, popular. Mary is his girlfriend—thinks she's lucky; doesn't want to lose him.
   b. Paul—wrong coat by mistake. Mary—didn't see any money. Stupid to ask questions after game—players tired.
   c. Jimmy could be the thief—no friends; wants money. Crying—frightened, guilty.
   d. Wrong to tell on friends—gets them into trouble. Mary doesn't know anything for sure.

C. What's your opinion?

1. Should Mary go to the principal or not? What else could she do?
2. Who could Mary ask for advice? Should she talk to Kate or not?
3. Do you think she should talk to Paul about the notice? Why or why not?
4. Why does Mary's mother think that Paul is a nice boy? Do *you* think he is?
5. Why is Paul more popular than Jimmy? Do you think Jimmy has a girlfriend?
6. How do you think Jimmy felt when he was called a thief?
7. What do you think the principal will do if no one comes to his office?

D. Talk it over.

1. What kinds of things get stolen in schools? Is it easy to find the thief?
2. What do people steal outside of schools? Why? How can they be stopped?
3. Can you explain why some people are more popular than others?
4. How should friends behave towards each other? What is a true friend?

E.

Imagine that Mary decides to talk to Paul about the missing money. Write the conversation which might take place. Ask another student to help you act it out during class.

21 Who makes the decisions?

Morgan Manufacturing, Inc.
St. Cloud, Minnesota 56372

```
Memo to:  All employees                    June 19, 1978
   From:  Carol Granger, Office Manager
   Re:    Employees' Association Meeting

A meeting of the Employees' Association will be held
in the Cafeteria on Wednesday, June 21, 1978, at 4:30 p.m.

Agenda

1.  Minutes of the meeting held on May 24, 1978
2.  Report of the Fourth of July Picnic Committee
3.  Debate: Should smoking be prohibited in all work areas?
4.  Other new business
```

25 Station Road
St. Cloud, Minn.
     56372
June 20, 1978

Dear María,

   I'm sorry I haven't written for so long. Last month I got a promotion. I'm now Office Manager and I am very busy! One of my new duties is to coordinate meetings of the Employees' Association. We have a big debate coming up tomorrow— "Should smoking be prohibited in work areas?" I know how I feel, but I can't offer my opinion. I'm just a referee.

   I've enclosed a copy of the memo about the meeting. I sound really official, don't I? I promise I'll write you a long letter next week.

                Love,
                Carol

A. Comprehension

1. Why hasn't Carol written to Maria for so long? Who *is* Maria?
2. What does Carol tell her about?
3. What does Carol enclose in the letter?
4. When and where will the meeting be held?
5. What's on the agenda?
6. What will Carol's position be during the meeting?

B. Should smoking be prohibited in all work areas?

1. *Present the argument for prohibiting smoking.*
   a. Uncomfortable for nonsmokers —can't breathe; eyes burn.
   b. Unhealthy—reports link smoking and cancer; may cause other diseases.
   c. Wastes time—smokers produce less; distracted from work.
   d. Dirty work area—matches, ashes, cigarette burns.

2. *State the argument for permitting smoking.*
   a. It's my own body—have a right to do as I wish.
   b. Cancer reports not conclusive; know smokers 90 years old.
   c. More productive—calm, happy, better able to concentrate.
   d. Can be clean—be careful; use ashtrays.
   e. Can't stop—smoked for years; impossible to stop; rather quit job.

C. Talk it over.

1. Do you smoke? If so, for how long have you smoked? Could you quit?
2. Is smoking allowed in your classrooms? In the halls? In the cafeteria? How do you feel about this?
3. Do you believe that smoking causes cancer? Why or why not?
4. Why do people start to smoke? What role does advertising play in this?
5. How much does it cost a person to smoke for one year? What else could he or she do with that money?

D.

Find out if there are classes or meetings in your community for people who want to stop smoking. When and where do they meet? How much do they cost?

22 The Young Scientist: Cruel or Curious?

Once there was a student who was very interested in spiders. Two things puzzled him. Spiders didn't seem to have any ears, and they had a lot of legs. One day he had an idea. Spiders must have extra legs so that they can hear. He discussed the idea with his biology teacher. "That's an interesting idea," said the teacher, "but you have to think of an experiment to prove it." So he did.

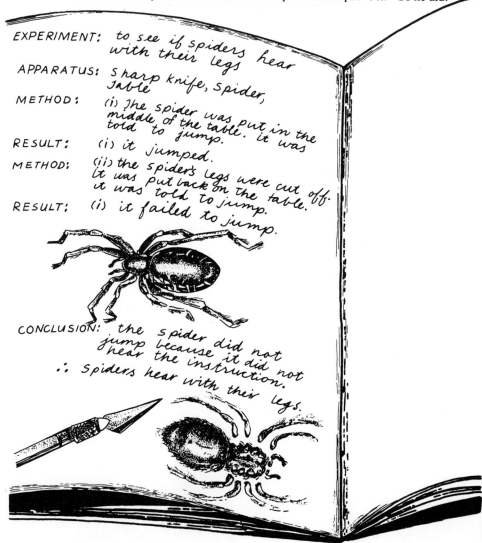

EXPERIMENT: to see if spiders hear with their legs

APPARATUS: Sharp knife, spider, table

METHOD: (i) The spider was put in the middle of the table. it was told to jump.

RESULT: (i) it jumped.

METHOD: (ii) the spider's legs were cut off. it was put back on the table. it was told to jump.

RESULT: (i) it failed to jump.

CONCLUSION: the spider did not jump because it did not hear the instruction. ∴ Spiders hear with their legs.

Did the student prove his theory? Is one experiment enough to prove anything?

A. Comprehension

1. Who was very interested in spiders? What puzzled him?
2. What idea did he have?
3. Who did he discuss it with?
4. What did he tell the student to do?
5. What was the aim of the biology student's experiment?
6. What apparatus did he use?
7. Describe the two parts of the experiment: the method and the results.
8. What conclusion did he draw from his experiment?
9. What did he really prove, if anything?
10. Do you think the spider felt pain?
11. Was the young scientist cruel or curious?

B. Should scientists experiment on living creatures?

1. *State the argument for such experiments.*
   a. Have to do experiments—can't find out facts any other way. Help us learn about life—how eyes, ears, muscles work.
   b. Interesting—more knowledge. Useful—help fight diseases, find cures. Test new drugs on animals—can't risk human life.
   c. Treat animals well, better than many pets—clean cages, good food, etc. Use animals no one wants; breed some specially.

2. *State the case against such experiments.*
   a. All creatures feel pain; wrong to breed animals to suffer. Scientists cruel, like small boys pulling wings off flies.
   b. Already know about life—no need for more experiments. Students can look up facts. More important to be kind than curious.
   c. Scientists selfish—should do experiments on selves. Wrong to use animals to cure humans—find volunteers.

C. Talk it over.

1. Do you do experiments in school? If so, what do you learn from them?
2. Why do people keep pets? How do they treat them?
3. The following creatures are used in scientific experiments: insects, frogs, mice, rabbits, guinea pigs, cats, dogs, monkeys, horses. Do you think some suffer more than others? Are scientists cruel? Should they use human volunteers instead? Could they?
4. Which is more important, to be kind to animals or to cure human diseases?
5. What do you know about these diseases: smallpox, malaria, cancer, polio, tuberculosis? What causes them? Can they be cured or prevented? How?

D. Would you volunteer? Why or why not?

What should schools teach?

Teacher

Politician

Principal

Moderator: This month our panel looks at education. Everyone seems to want more schools. But what *kind* of schools do we want?

Politician: Good ones, of course. My party believes that good schools make good citizens.

Principal: I prefer to talk about good *people*. In my school we aim to develop character. We try to teach students about right and wrong, and . . .

Mrs. Barnes: But that's the family's job! Schools should prepare children for their future careers.

Mr. Barnes: I agree. Teach useful subjects and help students pass exams.

Businessman: In my company we'd be happy if schools taught their students how to read, write and count properly! But teachers don't seem to care about the needs of industry.

Principal: Work is only one part of life. We feel we must educate students for leisure too. I'd like more art, music and physical education in the schedule.

Teacher: There's too much of that already. What about academic work? Schools should pass on knowledge from one generation to another.

Moderator: Well, we can't agree. I wonder what the students think.

Mr. Barnes

Mrs. Barnes

Businessman

A. Comprehension
1. What is the subject of this forum?
2. Do people agree about what kind of schools they want?
3. How many points of view are stated?
4. What does the politician believe?
5. How does the principal differ?
6. Why does Mrs. Barnes disagree?
7. What does her husband think?
8. Is the businessman satisfied with the job the schools are doing? Why or why not?
9. What would the principal like to see in the schedule?
10. Who disagrees with him? Why?
11. Can you suggest why the members of the panel disagree so much?
12. Who do you agree with most? Why?

B. What should schools teach?
Summarize the viewpoint of each member of the panel.
1. *The politician:* Good schools—good citizens.
2. *The principal:* Schools make good people—develop character; teach right and wrong; also educate for leisure, work only part of life—need more music, art, physical education.
3. *Mr. and Mrs. Barnes:* Family's job—teach right and wrong. School's job—teach useful subjects; help students pass exams; prepare students for future careers.
4. *The businessman:* Company wants people who can read, write, count—schools should teach basic skills; teachers don't care about industry's needs.
5. *The teacher:* Wants more academic work—too much art, music; schools should pass knowledge from one generation to another.

C. Talk it over.
1. How would you describe a good citizen? A good person?
2. How have you learned about right and wrong? Who should teach morals?
3. Which school subjects do you think are most useful? Why?
4. In what ways can schools prepare students for their future careers?
5. Who taught you how to read, write and count? Could people learn these basic skills if there were no schools? Why or why not?
6. Is it true that teachers don't care about industry's needs? If so, why?
7. Do you think people need to be educated for leisure? Why or why not?
8. What do *you* think schools should teach? What can they teach best?
9. At what age should students leave school? When does education end?

D. Fantasy schools
1. Make a list of subjects you'd like to study. Say why.
2. Allow 35 class periods a week. How much time would you give to each subject?
3. Plan a daily schedule to suit one of the members of the panel.

24 Equal Rights?

The Bell Family Charter

Housework   <u>All</u> members of the family must do an equal share of
             the housework according to age and ability. A list
             of duties will be put up each week.

Free Time   Children and parents have an equal right to free time.

Visitors   Children have a right to bring friends home whenever
             they like.

Bedtime   Bedtime will be fixed according to age.
             Children over fifteen may go to bed when they like.

Rules for   Parents must not break promises.
 Parents   Parents must not cancel plans suddenly.
             Parents must not criticize their children in public.

             N.B. Parents are not always right!

             Signed:

             Elizabeth Bell   (Mother, third grade teacher)
             Martin Bell   (Father, engineer)
             John Bell   (age sixteen, tenth grade student)
             Kate Bell   (age fourteen, eighth grade student)
             Andrew Bell   (age six, first grade student)

A. Comprehension

1. How many people are there in the Bell family?
2. What nationality are they? How do you know?
3. Who's the youngest?
4. What are the parents' jobs?
5. Do all the children go to school?
6. How is the housework divided?
7. How does each member of the family know which job to do?
8. Who gets the most free time?
9. How often can the children bring visitors home?
10. Can Andrew go to bed whenever he likes? Explain the rules about bedtime.
11. What are the rules for the parents?
12. Do the children think their parents never make mistakes?
13. Do the parents and children have equal rights? Why or why not?

B. What does the charter imply?

Do you agree or disagree with the following statements?
What are the arguments for and against each one?

1. Husbands should help their wives with the housework.
2. Married women have the right to go to work if they want.
3. Boys should do as much housework as girls.
4. Small children should be given jobs to do.
5. Children should be given as much free time as adults.
6. Children's friends are as important as their parents' friends.
7. Children over 15 are old enough to set their own bedtimes.
8. Parents must not do anything to upset their children.

C. What about *your* family?

1. Do you have any rules in your family? Who made them? What are they?
2. Who does the housework in your family? Do you help? Why or why not?
3. Who gets the most free time in your family? Why? How do your parents spend their free time? How do the children spend theirs?
4. Do you have rules about visitors? How do you entertain visitors?
5. What time do you go to bed? What about other members of your family?
6. Do family members ever criticize you? What for? Are they right?

D. Talk it over.

1. Why do people break promises or cancel plans suddenly? Have you ever had to? Is it always wrong to do so? Why or why not?
2. What duties do parents have that children don't?
3. How will/do you bring up your children?
4. Has family life changed in the past 50 years? If so, how? Tell what you know about family life in the past, and in other countries today.

E. Duty list

Can you work out a list of duties that would give an equal share of work to each member of the Bell family?

25 Motor Vehicles–
A Blessing or a Curse?

Picnic

Fire

Traffic jam

Car accident

A. Look at the pictures.

1. *Picnic*
   a. Describe the people in the picture.
   b. What are they doing?
   c. How did they get to the picnic?

2. *Fire*
   a. Is the fire engine new or old?
   b. How many firemen are there? What are they doing?
   c. What do they use the ladder for?

3. *Car accident*
   a. What kinds of vehicles can you see?
   b. How many people can you see? What are they doing?
   c. Can the car be driven away? Why or why not?
   d. Is it summer or winter? How do you know?
   e. What do you think happened?

4. *Traffic jam*
   a. How fast are the cars moving? How do you know?
   b. Where was the picture taken? How do you know?
   c. What time of day do you think it is? Why?

B. Motor vehicles—a blessing or a curse?

1. *State the positive aspects of motor vehicles.*
   a. Bring help quickly—police cars, fire engines, ambulances.
   b. Do important work—transport goods; deliver mail; take people to and from work.
   c. Convenient—door-to-door; comfortable; faster than trains, boats.
   d. Fun—take drives in country; take long vacations; enter races.

2. *State the negative aspects of motor vehicles.*
   a. Spoil cities—danger, noise, traffic jams.
   b. Pollute the air—give off lead, carbon dioxide.
   c. Spoil the countryside—take up land for roads; junkyards ugly.
   d. Eliminate exercise—healthier to walk, ride bicycles.
   e. Must be controlled—expensive, ugly, unhealthy.

C. What's your opinion?

1. Do you think motor vehicles have improved life or not? Give your reasons.
2. Which do you think is the best way to travel—by car, by train, on a bicycle, on foot? Tell why you feel this way.
3. Do you think cars are beautiful or ugly? What about other motor vehicles?
4. Do you think motor vehicles spoil the countryside? Why or why not?
5. Can you suggest how to stop car accidents? Traffic jams?

D. Talk it over.

1. Does your family own a car? If so, what do you use it for?
2. Have you ever seen a car accident or a fire? Describe what happened.
3. Would you like to be a policeman or an ambulance driver? Give your reasons.

E.

What two items are most important when buying a car: price, looks, safety, economy, size? Give reasons for your choices.

26 **Foolish or** Fashionable?

Susan: Oh Dad, I've been invited to a party on Saturday.
Mr. Brown: How nice. Where is it?
Susan: At the Winters' house. It's a formal party so I'll need a new dress.
Mr. Brown: What's wrong with the last one you bought? You've only worn it twice.

Susan: But everyone's seen it!
Mr. Brown: Well, they'll have to see it again. I can't afford to buy you a new dress every month. I'm not made of money.
Susan: But Dad, I don't buy many new clothes.
Mr. Brown: Honestly, Susan. Don't they teach you anything at school? Hundreds of girls *never* get any new clothes. In many parts of the world, your weekly allowance would have to feed a whole family.
Susan: I don't care.
Mr. Brown: Well, I do. You're very selfish, and you're foolish about money. That's why I'm not going to buy you a new dress. I'm going to give the money to charity instead.

A. Comprehension
1. What has Susan been invited to?
2. Why does Susan want a new dress?
3. What does her father think she should wear?
4. Why does Susan disagree?
5. Why can't her father afford to buy her new dresses every month?
6. Does Susan buy many new clothes?
7. How much does she know about life in poorer families?
8. Why does her father say she's foolish about money?
9. Why does he think she's selfish?

B. Foolish or fashionable?
1. *State Susan's point of view.*
   a. Need a new dress—party at Winters' house; formal; everyone's seen other dress.
   b. Father doesn't understand—could easily afford a new dress. Don't buy many new clothes.
   c. Talks of other girls—no new clothes; other countries—no money for food. I don't care—I can't help them.

2. *State Mr. Brown's point of view.*
   a. Susan wants new dress—formal party; just bought new dress; worn twice; can wear it again.
   b. Can't buy new dresses every month—Susan's foolish about money.
   c. She's ignorant, selfish—many girls never get new clothes; her spending money would feed a family. Give money to charity, not Susan.

C. What's your opinion?
1. Do you think Susan needs a new dress? Why or why not?
2. If her father *can* afford to buy her a new dress, should he refuse?
3. Why do hundreds of girls never get any new clothes? Do *you* care?
4. How much spending money do you think Susan gets? Do you think she saves any?
5. Do you think Susan is selfish? Why or why not? Can her father make her care about poorer people? Did he do the right thing?

D. Talk it over.
1. What kind of clothes are fashionable at the present time? Do you think some women and girls are too interested in fashion? What about some men and boys?
2. What is a reasonable amount of spending money? Do girls need more than boys? Should older children get more than younger ones?
3. Should children give money to charity? Talk about a charity that you are familiar with.
4. Why are some countries richer than others? Why do some families have more money than others? Can anything be done about it? What do you think should be done?

E. A proverb
Charity begins at home.
Do you agree? Explain.

27   What kind of mind do you have?

Psychologists study our minds to find out how we think. They have discovered that people have a variety of mental abilities. Some people are good at solving problems stated in words; they have good verbal ability. Others are better at problems involving numbers and shapes; they have good nonverbal ability.

Verbal Question: Which word is unlike the others?
a. eye b. nose c. foot d. mouth e. ear

Nonverbal Question: $5 + X = 21$ $X = ?$
a. 5 b. 20 c. 26 d. 12 e. 16

The answers to the above questions are c and e. What are your abilities? What kind of mind do you have? Do you have better verbal or nonverbal ability? Below is a short test to help you find out. Write your answers on a piece of paper. Do the test as quickly as you can.

1. One shape is unlike the others. Which is it?
   a. ▽ b. ☐ c. △ d. ◁ e. ▷
2. One number is unlike the others. Which is it?
   a. 3 b. 5 c. 7 d. 8 e. 11
3. One word is unlike the others. Which is it?
   a. bed b. table c. chair d. fork e. desk
4. Which shape should come in the middle?
   a. ...   b. .   c. ∴   d. ..   e. .∵.
5. Which number should come in the middle?
   a. 3924 b. 3942 c. 3492 d. 3429 e. 3294
6. Which word should come in the middle?
   a. house b. country c. city d. state e. street
7. Complete the following:
   ☐ is to ◨ as ◩ is to _____.
   a. ⊠ b. ◪ c. ◨ d. ⊟ e. ◪
8. Complete the following:
   5 is to 25 as 7 is to _____.
   a. 14 b. 17 c. 21 d. 28 e. 35
9. Complete the following:
   Flower is to rose as tree is to _____.
   a. forest b. oak c. tree d. trunk e. red
10. One shape is unlike the others. Which is it?
    a. ◰ b. ◧ c. ◼ d. ⊞ e. ◪
11. 1, 4, _____, 10, 13. What number is missing?
    a. 5 b. 6 c. 7 d. 8 e. 9
12. One word is unlike the others. Which is it?
    a. to b. the c. in d. on e. at

(Answers on page 61.)

A. Look at your score.
1. 1, 4, 7 and 10 are shape problems; 2, 5, 8 and 11 are number problems; 3, 6, 9 and 12 are word problems. Which type of problem did you do best on?
2. Which did you find easier—the verbal problems (3, 6, 9, 12) or the nonverbal problems (1, 2, 4, 5, 7, 8, 10, 11)? Are you a verbal or nonverbal thinker?
3. A student with a low verbal score might find English and history classes difficult. A student with a low nonverbal score might experience difficulty in math and science classes. Do these statements hold true in your case?

B. Some psychologists think students can be divided into two types.

	1. *Type one*	2. *Type two*
Test Scores	Poor on 1, 2, 4, 5, 7, 8, 10, 11; good on 3, 6, 9, 12.	Good on 1, 2, 4, 5, 7, 8, 10, 11; poor on 3, 6, 9, 12.
Type of ability	Verbal	Nonverbal
Accuracy	Probably low	Probably high
Best subjects	History, English, art	Physics, math
Worst subjects	Math, science	English, history
Vocabulary	Extensive	Limited
Interests	Literature, art	Cars, radio building
Career goal	Journalism	Engineering

C. What about you?
1. In which subjects is it most important to be accurate? Are you accurate in those subjects?
2. What are your best and worst subjects? Why are you good at some and bad at others?
3. What are your special interests?
4. Which type of student do you think you are? What about your friends?

D. Talk it over.
1. What are your career goals?
2. Which do you think is most important for success in school?
   a. a good memory   b. intelligence   c. hard work   d. imagination
3. Which of the following need a wide vocabulary? Good math skills? Why?
   a. lawyers   b. carpenters   c. engineers   d. composers
   e. teachers
4. Are the following statements true? How could you find out?
   a. People are more intelligent at 15 than at 50.
   b. Men are more intelligent than women.

E. Give the test on page 53 to a friend. Are your friend's abilities mainly verbal or nonverbal? What jobs would your friend be good at?

28 Focus on Work

"An army marches on its stomach," said Napoleon. The great general believed that people couldn't work when they were hungry. They didn't have any energy. So he tried to give his soldiers plenty to eat. Our knowledge has advanced since then. Scientists can now measure the amount of energy that different kinds of food provide.* They can also calculate how much food different people require. How much food do *you* need? That depends on your age, sex, size and on the work you do. The harder you work, the more food you need. What kind of work requires the most energy? Scientists have studied this too. Look at the following chart.

Daily calorie requirements

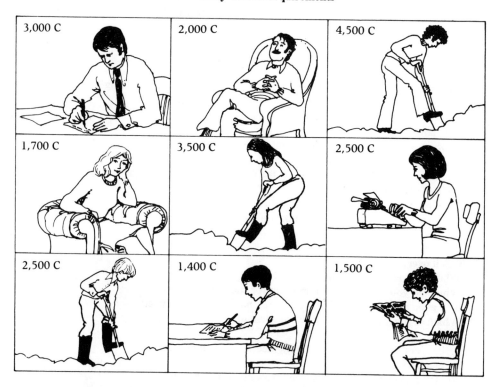

* 1 calorie = the amount of heat needed to raise the temperature of 1 gram of water by 1° centigrade.

A. Comprehension

1. Who was Napoleon? Why did he give his soldiers plenty to eat?
2. What can scientists now measure?
3. What can they calculate?
4. What does the amount of food a person needs depend on?
5. What else have scientists studied?
6. What is the title of the chart?
7. How many calories a day does the man writing require?
8. Which man needs the most calories?
9. Which woman needs the fewest? Why?
10. What about the children? Which activity is most energetic?
11. Would you expect writing or typing to use more energy? Why?
12. Why does the man writing need more calories than the woman typing?
13. Who needs the most calories when digging? Why?
14. Which activities are mental and which are physical?

B. Are the following statements true or false? Give your reasons.

1. The chart tells how many calories it takes to do various jobs.
2. The chart shows that children don't work as hard as adults.
3. The chart proves that physical work is harder than mental work.
4. The chart shows that men, women and children need different amounts of food.
5. The chart shows that some activities use more energy than others.
6. The chart proves that men work harder than women.
7. The chart shows that calorie requirements are highest for people who use their muscles in their jobs.
8. The chart shows that it is easier to measure physical work than mental work.
9. The chart explains why fat people go on diets and do exercises.

C. What's your opinion?

1. What's *your* definition of work? Is it what you are paid to do? Is it what you spend most of your time doing?
2. You use energy to play tennis. Why isn't tennis work? Or is it?
3. What kind of work can machines do for us? Have machines improved life?
4. Have you studied physics? What do physicists mean by work?
5. Do you think scientists *can* measure work? Why or why not?
6. Would *you* rather work with your muscles or with your mind? Why?
7. Would people be happier if they didn't have to work? Why or why not?

D. Argue for or against the following statements.

1. Women should get equal pay for equal work.
2. People who do heavy manual work should get paid more than office workers.

E. A quotation from Mencius, a Chinese philosopher of the 4th century B.C.

"There are those who use their minds and there are those who use their muscles. The former rule; the latter are ruled."
Has the world changed?

29 Examinations are a necessary evil

David is talking to his younger sister, Ellen.

Ellen: Hello, David. How was the English exam?
David: All right. Mr. Marks tried to be funny. Look at the first question.

Ellen: Did you do it?
David: As a matter of fact, I did. I could think of plenty to say about the evils of exams! I haven't had a good night's sleep in weeks.
Ellen: But the question suggests that exams are *necessary* too. What did you say about that?
David: Oh, I thought of a few things. Here, look at my notes. They're on the back.

English 101
Final Examination
Dr. Frank Marks

Time allowed: 2¹/₂ hours
Answer all sections on this paper.
Write a 250-word composition on one of the following subjects.

SECTION A: COMPOSITION

1. Examinations are a necessary evil.
2. Dangerous sports should be abolished.

EXAMS

Necessary (pros)   Evil (cons)
make you work   divide people into pass or fail
help you get jobs   can't do your best — nerves

Ellen: Is that all? You could have said lots more. Why didn't you suggest an alternative to exams?
David: Oh, come on, Ellen. As soon as you enter the room, your mind goes blank. Wait till it's your turn. Anyway, let's not talk about it anymore. I've got to review 200 years of history before tomorrow.

A. Comprehension
1. What was David telling Ellen about?
2. What did he think of the exam questions?
3. Which composition subject did he choose? Why?
4. What did Ellen notice about the first question?
5. Did she think David had answered the question well?
6. What did she think he should have suggested?
7. What was David's excuse?
8. Why did he change the subject?

B. Are examinations a necessary evil?
1. *State the positive aspects of exams.*
   a. Necessary—make you work; show who's studied; help select people for college, jobs, etc.
   b. Fair—same time, same questions for all. Standardized exams—no names; marked by strangers; *what* you know, not *who* you know, for jobs, etc.
   c. Preparation for life—need ability to think quickly, good memory. Do well in exams—succeed in life.

2. *State the negative aspects of exams.*
   a. Evil—test memory, not understanding of subject; learn facts, not principles. Can't do your best—nerves, time limits, etc.
   b. Unfair—some people can't work quickly; a year's work in an hour. Examiners don't see best work—rest of life may depend on one day.
   c. Divide people—pass and fail. In life we need ability to work steadily, to help others.

C. For further discussion
1. What do *you* think of exams? Would you like to abolish them?
2. If you didn't have exams, do you think you would work harder, or not? How would your study habits change?
3. What do your friends and teachers think of exams?
4. What advice would you give a friend before an important examination?
5. How do *you* think people should be selected for universities, jobs, etc.?
6. What kinds of tests do people have to face in life outside of school? Is it true that people who do well on exams succeed in later life? If so, why?
7. What are some alternatives to traditional examinations?

D. How to improve exams
Here's one idea. Allow students to take notes and books into examinations. Then they can demonstrate understanding, instead of just the ability to memorize. What do you think about this? Can you suggest other ideas?

30 School vacations are too long

JUNE							JULY						
S	M	T	W	T	F	S	S	M	T	W	T	F	S
○ FM 1 30	☾ LQ 8	● NM 16	1	2	3	4	☾ LQ 7	● NM 16	☽ IQ 23	( ) FM 30		1	2
5	6	7	8	9	10	11	3	4	5	6	7	8	9
12	13	14	15	16	⑰	18	10	11	12	13	14	15	16
19	20	21	22	23	24	25	17	18	19	20	21	22	23
26	27	28	29	30		☽ LQ 24	24 31	25	26	27	28	29	30

AUGUST							SEPTEMBER						
S	M	T	W	T	F	S	S	M	T	W	T	F	S
☾ LQ 6	1	2	3	4	5	6	☾ LQ 5	● NM 13	☽ IQ 20	( ) FM 27	1	2	3
7	8	9	10	11	12	13	4	5	6	⑦	8	9	10
14	15	16	17	18	19	20	11	12	13	14	15	16	17
21	22	23	24	25	26	27	18	19	20	21	22	23	24
28	29	30	31	● NM 14	☽ IQ 21	( ) FM 28	25	26	27	28	29	30	

Dear Editor:

Today the children finally returned to school. After more than two months' vacation, they have started their fall term. How many adults get such a long vacation? Two to four weeks plus national holidays—that's what the working man gets. As for the average woman, she's lucky to get a vacation at all.

Children don't need such long vacations. Their daily hours are shorter than anyone else's. During vacations most of them get bored, and some of them get into trouble. What a waste! If their overworked parents were given more free time instead, everyone would be happier.

This isn't just a national problem either—it's worldwide. Dates may be different from country to country, but the pattern is the same. Why should children do half as much work and get twice as much vacation as their parents?

Mrs. Pat Walker
Mother of four
Philadelphia, Pennsylvania

59

A. Comprehension

1. What is Mrs. Walker complaining about?
2. When did she write her complaint?
3. Do children or adults get longer vacations?
4. How much vacation does the working man get?
5. What about the average woman?
6. Why does Mrs. Walker think that children don't need long vacations?
7. Why does she want adults to have more free time?
8. What is the extent of the problem?
9. How do different countries compare?
10. What is Mrs. Walker's final point?

B. Are school vacations too long?

1. *State Mrs. Walker's argument.*
   a. School vacations are too long—children, over two months; men, two to four weeks; women, lucky to get any vacation.
   b. Children don't need long vacations—short daily hours; get bored, get in trouble during vacations.
   c. Waste—parents more free time; everyone happier. World problem—dates different, pattern the same. Children—half the work, twice the vacation time.

2. *Construct a counter-argument.*
   a. Children need long vacations—time to rest, play, visit relatives, travel to places of interest, develop hobbies.
   b. Schoolwork hard—learning new things; homework. Adults —men do the same thing all day; women stay home. Children don't get paid.
   c. Most children enjoy vacations. Mrs. Walker jealous, tired.
   d. *Teachers* need vacations.

C. What's your opinion?

1. Do you think school vacations are too long? Do you get bored? Why or why not?
2. Why do you think Mrs. Walker felt angry about the school vacations?
3. How much vacation time does the average worker get in this country? Is it enough? How does he or she spend it?
4. Why do some workers get longer vacations than others?
5. Do you agree that the average woman is lucky to get a vacation at all?
6. Who needs the longest vacation: men, women or children? Give reasons for your answer.
7. Why do different countries have different dates for school vacations?
8. Do you think parents need more free time? Would it make them happier?
9. Do you think teachers need more vacation than other adults? Why or why not?

D. Talk it over.

1. What did you do during your last vacation? What are you planning to do during your next one? Describe the best vacation you've ever had.
2. Is it easy to plan a vacation trip to suit all the members of the family? Why or why not?
3. When are the national holidays in this country? How do people spend them?

E. A proverb

A change is as good as a rest. Do you agree or disagree? Why?

Answer Page

Lesson One

C. What would an interviewer think of you?

Give yourself 5 points for each "a," 4 points for a "b," 3 points for a "c," 2 points for a "d" and 0 points for an "e."

Totals: 16–20   Interviewer very impressed
        11–15   Interviewer pleased
        6–10   Interviewer doubtful
        0– 5   Interviewer very doubtful

Lesson Six

E.   What's your score?

1. b   2. c   3. c

Lesson Eight

E. Water quiz

1. Hydrogen and oxygen (H_2O)   2. About 50%   3. a) 2; b) 1; c) 3

Lesson Twelve

The Farmers' Market opens at noon and Bates said he arrived at his sister's house at noon. He couldn't have bought the flowers at the Farmers' Market. He could have taken Northern Blvd. to Bayside, committed the crime and then gotten back on the expressway and driven to Smithtown.

Lesson Sixteen

E.   Telegraph, telephone, radio, television

Lesson Twenty-Seven

Test

1. b	2. d	3. d	4. a	5. c
6. c	7. a	8. e	9. b	10. d
11. c	12. b			

Some Useful Phrases

A. Expressing a personal point of view

1. In my opinion . . .
2. Personally, I think . . .
3. I'd say that . . .
4. In my experience . . .
5. As far as I'm concerned . . .
6. Speaking for myself . . .
7. I'd suggest that . . .
8. I'd like to point out that . . .
9. I believe that . . .
10. What I mean is . . .

B. Agreeing with someone else's point of view

1. Exactly.
2. Yes, I agree.
3. Of course.
4. That's true.
5. So do I. (Neither do I.)
6. I think so too. (I don't think so either.)
7. You're (absolutely) right.
8. I agree with you entirely.
9. That's a good point.
10. I go along with that.

C. Disagreeing with someone else's point of view

1. However . . .
2. On the other hand . . .
3. On the contrary . . .
4. I don't agree with you.
5. I'm afraid I have to disagree.
6. I'm sorry to disagree with you, but . . .
7. That's not (entirely) true.
8. Yes, but don't you think . . .?
9. That's different.
10. That's not the same thing at all.